My Little Christmas Prayer Book

by Maïte Roche

CTS Children's Books

In the name of the Father
and of the Son and of the Holy Spirit.

Soon it will be Christmas!
Day after day,
Jesus, I wait for you,
and I'm getting ready for your coming.
We will have a party to celebrate your birth.
Come to us, Jesus,
we are ready to welcome you,
light up our hearts,
they are full of love for you.
Come, Lord Jesus!

Amen.

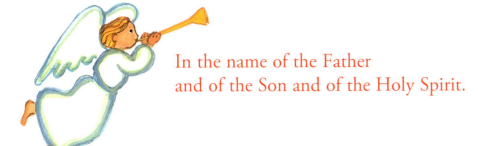

In the name of the Father
and of the Son and of the Holy Spirit.

Thank you, my God.
Thank you, loving Father,
for Jesus, your beloved Son.
With the Angels, I sing of your wonders:
"Glory to God in the highest
and peace on earth
to the people he loves!
Glory to God! Glory to God!"

Amen.

In the name of the Father
and of the Son and of the Holy Spirit.

Noel, Noel!
Joy to the world, the Lord is come!
Jesus, we are coming to you
to celebrate and sing for joy.
Guide our steps with your light!
Jesus, we are coming to you.
A Child is born this day for us!
Happy Christmas!

Amen.

In the name of the Father
and of the Son and of the Holy Spirit.

Jesus, little baby
lying in the manger,
close to Mary and Joseph,
you are looking at us
and you love us.
Together with the astonished shepherds
on Christmas night,
Jesus, I am looking at you and I love you.

Amen.

In the name of the Father
and of the Son and of the Holy Spirit.

Thank you, Lord,
for Christmas Day.
It's so good to be loved!
Thank you, Lord,
for this day of celebration.
It's so good to share
the happiness you give us!

Amen.

In the name of the Father
and of the Son and of the Holy Spirit.

Here are the Magi
who followed the star
to come and adore you and offer you
gold, frankincense and myrrh.
You are the Lord,
the King of the universe and the King of hearts.
You have come to gather together
all the people on earth
in the love of God
our Father.

Amen.

In the name of the Father
and of the Son and of the Holy Spirit.

Jesus,
Mary and Joseph,
God's Holy Family,
Bless my Daddy and Mummy
and all my family and everyone I love.
May the peace and joy of Christmas
come to our home
and fill the whole
wide world!

Amen.

CTS Children's Books

The Beautiful Story of Jesus, by Maïte Roche (CTS Code CH 13)
The Beautiful Story of the Bible, by Maïte Roche (CTS Code CH 27)
The Bible for little children, by Maïte Roche (CTS Code CH 2)
First prayers for little children, by Maïte Roche (CTS Code CH 5)
The Gospel for little children, by Maïte Roche (CTS Code CH 1)
The most beautiful Christmas Story, by Maïte Roche (CTS Code CH 8)
My Little Christmas Prayer Book, by Maïte Roche (CTS Code CH 31)
My Little Missal, by Maïte Roche (CTS Code CH 20)

Text and illustrations by Maïte Roche
Translated by Helena Scott

My Little Christmas Prayer Book: Published 2010 by The Incorporated Catholic Truth Society, 40-46 Harleyford Road, London SE11 5AY. Tel: 020 7640 0042; Fax: 020 7640 0046; www.cts-online.org.uk. Copyright © 2010 The Incorporated Catholic Truth Society in this English-language edition.

ISBN: 978 1 86082 701 3   CTS Code CH 31

Original title **Premières prières pour Noel**: ISBN 978-2-7289-1317-6 © Fleurus-Mame, 2009.